IN THE COUNTRYSIDE

This I-SPY book belongs to:_____

I-SPY

Introduction

The British countryside is beautiful, and fascinating as any in the world. Since people first occupied these islands, more than 10,000 years ago, they have left their marks and traces on the land. As well as woods, forest and farms, there are miles of byways and footpaths contained by different kinds of fencing and gated by different kinds of barriers, where even a dog may have its own special access. Every part of the British countryside has its own particular character so as you stroll through across the fields or walk through country lanes, keep on the lookout and you might be surprised to discover just how much there is to I-Spy in the Country.

We are proud to have worked closely on this title with The Woodland Trust, the UK's leading woodland conservation charity.

The Woodland Trust has over 1,000 woods across the UK which you are welcome to visit for free. As well as looking after woodland and its wildlife, the Trust not only plants trees but encourages people to have a go at planting a tree too, as part of its More Trees, More Good project.

As well as I-Spying in the countryside, you can play and explore with ideas galore! Fun, fresh and FREE the Woodland Trust's nature detectives website has over a thousand downloads and activities to help you discover nature, woods and trees. Start your own adventure at www.naturedetectives.org.uk

The Trust's nature detectives CLUB is packed full with even more – get stickers, a giant wall chart, seasonal activity packs stuffed with ideas, plus new nature challenges every single week. Perfect for inquisitive I-Spyers! Dig in at www.naturedetectives.org.uk/club or call 0800 026 9650

How to use your I-SPY book

As you work through this book, you will notice that the subjects are arranged in groups or activities which are related to the seasons or kind of places where you are likely to find things. You need 1000 points to send off for your I-Spy certificate (see page 64) but that is not too difficult because there are masses of points in every book. As you make each I-Spy, write your score in the box.

SOFT MOSS

There are hundreds of different types of mosses. They like moisture, clean air and can grow on rocks, trees and buildings.

 I - SPY points: 10

PRICKLY TEASEL

This spiky flower head is covered with hundreds of purple flowers during June to October which attract bees and butterflies. When the flowers die, just the prickly head remains and it makes a great natural paintbrush (but watch out for the thorns on the stem).

 I - SPY points: 15

FLAKY LICHEN

Lichens are affected by the quality of the air. Many will only grow where there is clean air, whilst some prefer the nitrogen found in polluted air.

 I - SPY points: 15

STICKY GOOSEGRASS

This common hedgerow plant is covered in tiny hooks that help it stick to passing animals to spread its seeds. It also means it sticks to clothing and skin – this makes it great for sneakily sticking on people!

I - SPY points: 10

 Texture Trail
Double your points on this page – try out the texture trail at:
www.naturedetectives.org.uk/ispy

SILKY FORGET-ME-NOT PETALS

These tiny blue or purple flowers grow in clumps in spring. A German legend says when God named all of the plants, a tiny flower cried out "Forget-me-not, oh Lord!" and that became its name.

I - SPY points: 10

TICKLY FEATHER

Feathers help birds fly, keep warm and can protect them from water. Some birds have feathers that camouflage them so they can hide from predators, whilst others are brightly coloured or patterned to help them attract mates.

 I - SPY points: 10

PAPERY SYCAMORE SEED

Sycamore seeds are also known as 'helicopters' because of the way they float and spin in the wind. The seeds have adapted to this shape to spread their seeds.

I - SPY points: 5

WET RAINDROP

Every minute of the day around 900 million tonnes of rain falls on the earth – that's equivalent to the weight of 130 million double-decker buses!

 I - SPY points: 5

LACY LEAF SKELETON

Deciduous trees like oak, beech and lime shed their leaves in autumn. These leaves provide shelter and food for all sorts of minibeasts. They gradually break down over time, usually the fleshy parts of the leaf first, leaving a 'skeleton' behind.

 I - SPY points: 15

CRUMBLY SOIL FROM A MOLEHILL

Molehills are made by moles tunnelling underground, pushing up earth as they hunt for earthworms. They have spade-like front paws which are ideal for digging tunnels and they can tunnel up to 20m (65ft) a day!

I - SPY points: 15

HOOTING TAWNY OWL

The Tawny Owl is Britain's most common woodland owl (although it is not found in Ireland). The famous 't-wit t-woo' sound is actually created by two tawny owls, a female and a male, calling to each other.

 I - SPY points: 20

CHIRPING GRASSHOPPER

Have you ever wandered along a grass verge or through a field in summer and heard the air buzzing with chirping grasshoppers? Grasshoppers make this noise by rubbing their hindlegs against their forewings.

 I - SPY points: 10

WOODLAND TRUST

MICHELIN

RAT A TAT WOODPECKER

You may hear male great spotted woodpeckers 'drumming' in spring, either to attract a mate or to warn off other male woodpeckers. Both males and females chisel out holes in tree trunks to make nests, or peck at the bark looking for insects with their long tongues.

 I - SPY points: 30

Sounds
Go on a sound safari to double your points on this page. Print a tick sheet at *www.naturedetectives.org.uk/ispy*

RIBBITING FROG

Some people believe frogs and toads are particularly sensitive to weather changes and croak louder when rain or a storm is on the way. Test this out next time you're near a pond.

 I - SPY points: 20

STINKHORN FUNGUS

The stinkhorn fungus is well-named! It has a slimy, olive-green cap containing its spores. The slime smells like rotting meat and attracts flies which then carry the spores away on their legs.

I - SPY points: 30

HONEYSUCKLE

This climbing plant wraps itself around other shrubs and trees. It blooms in summer, with the flowers smelling their sweetest and strongest in the evening.

I - SPY points: 10

WILD GARLIC

This plant flowers in spring and fills woodlands with its strong garlic scent. Wild boar like to dig up the bulbs and eat them.

I - SPY points: 15

 Surprising Smells
Double up! Complete the surprising smells hunt at *www.naturedetectives.org.uk/ispy* to double your points on this page.

GORSE

Gorse is actually a member of the pea family! It flowers for most of the year and its bright yellow flower heads smell strongly of coconut. (Just watch your nose on its sharp thorny spines).

I - SPY points: 15

BLACKBERRIES

Blackberries come from the bramble plant, ripening in late summer when they're perfect for picking. Birds, badgers, mice and butterflies are also fond of nibbling this juicy fruit.

I - SPY points: 5

Foraging
Lots of woodland plants are poisonous, so never eat anything without asking an adult first.

SWEET CHESTNUTS

It is thought the Sweet Chestnut tree was brought to the UK by the Romans over 2,000 years ago. The chestnuts are hidden inside a prickly case and are traditionally roasted and eaten at Christmas-time. They can also be ground down into flour and used to make bread or cakes.

I - SPY points: 5

WOODLAND TRUST

 MICHELIN

ELDERFLOWERS

The elder tree flowers in early summer and the blossom is commonly used to make cordial and champagne. The flower heads can also be deep-fried to make 'fritters'.

I - SPY points: 10

 Blackberry Pack
Download a free blackberry pack crammed with yummy recipes at *www.naturedetectives.org.uk/ispy* Make a tasty treat to double your points on this page.

ROSEHIPS

Rosehips are bursting with vitamin C. During the war people were paid to collect them to turn into syrup as other fruits were hard to get hold of. The seeds also contain tiny hairs which make a fantastic itching powder!

I - SPY points: 5

SPRING COLOUR

The UK is home to the world's best bluebell displays – they appear in spring, often growing so close together they look like a shimmering blue carpet.

 I - SPY points: 10

SUMMER COLOUR

Wildflower meadows are home to lots of wildlife including butterflies, bees and grasshoppers. They usually include a colourful mix of wildflowers, such as poppies, ox-eye daisies and cornflowers.

 I - SPY points: 10

WOODLAND TRUST

MICHELIN

AUTUMN COLOUR

The colourful autumn displays of broad-leaved trees vary depending on sunlight, rain and temperature. A bright, sunny autumn will usually lead to the most dazzling displays.

I - SPY points: 10

 Seasonal Spotter Sheets
Double your points on this page – download a seasonal spotter sheet and tick off all of the spots
www.naturedetectives.org.uk/ispy

WINTER

A hoar frost makes everything looks as if it has been coated with a layer of sparkling ice crystals. It occurs in very cold temperatures when water vapour in the air condenses onto surfaces that are below freezing, forming ice crystals.

I - SPY points: 10

SPLASH IN A MUDDY PUDDLE

It's great fun splashing about in your wellies, but animals like muddy puddles too. Swallows sometimes use mud from puddles to build their nests and some species of butterflies drink from muddy puddles to get extra salts and minerals they can't get from nectar.

 I - SPY points: 5

BALANCE ON A LOG

Fallen branches and logs are brilliant for balancing on. As they decay, the dead wood is also a vital habitat for many creatures and fungi providing food, shelter and a place to breed, but be careful – they can be slippery.

 I - SPY points: 5

WEAVE IN AND OUT OF TREES

Planting trees either side of paths or roads has been very popular for hundreds of years. Clumber Park in Nottinghamshire has the longest double planted lime avenue in Europe – 3.2km (two miles) long and made up of 1,296 trees, all around 170 years old.

 I - SPY points: 5

KICK THROUGH LEAVES

Watch out for dazzling displays in autumn as the leaves on deciduous trees turn yellow, orange and gold before falling to the ground. The colours vary depending on how warm and dry the summer and autumn weather is.

 I - SPY points: 5

HUG A HUGE, OLD TREE

The Woodland Trust's Ancient Tree Hunt records the UK's old and interesting trees. It uses hugs to measure how big their trunks are. Find the biggest tree you can – how many hugs big is it? Record it at www.AncientTreeHunt.org.uk

 I - SPY points: 15

CRAWL THROUGH LONG GRASS

Patches of long grass are great places to look for minibeasts. You can encourage bugs in your garden by leaving a corner to go 'wild' – if you stop cutting the grass and create a wood pile you might also attract frogs, toads and hedgehogs too.

 I - SPY points: 10

>
> **Play**
> Download a free play booklet to double your points on this page at
> *www.naturedetectives.org.uk/ispy*

HIDE BEHIND OR IN A HUGE TREE

Trees are fantastic for hide and seek. As they grow older some become hollow, like the Bowthorpe Oak in Lincolnshire which can fit 39 people inside! Can you find a hollow tree to hide in?

 I - SPY points: 15

FIND A FACE IN THE TREES

Take a closer look at the trees around you, can you see any faces looking back? Knobbly growths, gnarled roots and dark animal tunnels underneath trees often look like eyes, noses and mouths.

 I - SPY points: 20

TREE-CLIMBING

The best trees for climbing are big ones like oak, beech and ash. Look for healthy looking ones with plenty of strong branches at regular intervals. A good tip is to climb near the trunk, where the branches are strongest, but take care not to fall off!

I - SPY points: 15

> **Build a Den**
> Build a den in the woods to double your points on this page. Watch the video online to get ideas
> *www.naturedetectives.org.uk/ispy*

DEN BUILDING

Can you find a secret shelter hidden in the woods? Make your own with fallen branches, grass and leaves – what can you find to make it waterproof and windproof?

I - SPY points: 20

CENTIPEDE

Centipedes don't actually have 100 legs, it's usually only between 30-40 legs. You can tell them apart from millipedes because centipedes only have one pair of legs on each segment of their body, unlike millipedes which have two pairs, this makes centipedes better adapted for running. Centipedes have poisonous claws which they use to attack and capture prey.

 I - SPY points: 10

GREEN SHIELD BUG

The green shield bug gets its name from the colour and shape of its body. It is also sometimes called a 'green stink bug' because it gives out a terrible smell if handled or disturbed. Green shield bugs turn brown just before they hibernate for winter, then they turn back to green when they wake up in spring.

 I - SPY points: 25

SNAIL

Snails are one of the slowest species on earth – the garden snail is the fastest type of snail, with a top speed around 50 metres (164 yards) per hour. Snails are also extremely strong and can lift up to 10 times their own body weight!

 I - SPY points: 5

EARTHWORM

Earthworms help to recycle decaying plant matter by eating it and turning it into fertile soil, by loosening and mixing up the soil they also help to bring nutrients closer to the surface.

 **I - SPY** points: 5

LACEWING

Lacewings get their name from the delicate network of veins in their transparent wings, which look like lace. Both adults and larvae are carnivorous – the larvae suck the juice from aphids, then hide under the drained bodies to creep up on unsuspecting prey!

 **I - SPY** points: 10

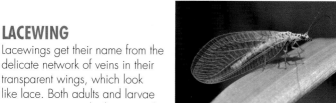

7 SPOT LADYBIRD

Ladybirds are brightly-coloured to warn predators they don't taste very nice. They can also release drops of strong smelling, yellow liquid to warn off potential predators. Both adult ladybirds and the larvae eat aphids, a big pest in gardens, so ladybirds are a great friend to gardeners.

 I - SPY points: 10

MinibeastiDial
Double up! Make a minibeast iDial to identify creepy crawlies and double your points on this page
www.naturedetectives.org.uk/ispy

ANT

They are very strong and can lift up to 50 times their own body weight. This is because ants have a different muscle structure to humans, if you had the same muscle structure as an ant you would be able to lift a car above your head!

 I - SPY points: 10

22

SPECKLED WOOD BUTTERFLY

You'll find this butterfly in woods, gardens and hedgerows. The adults rarely drink nectar from flowers, preferring instead to feed on honeydew secreted by aphids. Male speckled wood butterflies are particularly territorial so you'll often see them circling up into the air and clashing wings in battle.

 I - SPY points: 25

WOODLOUSE

Woodlice belong to the crustacean family and are more closely related to crabs and shrimps than other insects. You'll find them in damp, dark places like under rocks and logs, as well as compost heaps.

 I - SPY points: 5

5-SPOT BURNET MOTH

The 5-spot burnet moth is one of the few moths that fly during the day. It is very distinctive with black wings and five red spots on each wing. The bright colouring acts as a warning to potential predators that the moth tastes awful.

 I - SPY points: 25

WATER BOATMAN

Water boatmen are commonly found in ponds, lakes and slow-moving rivers. They use their long back legs like oars to propel them through the water, so they look a bit like tiny rowing boats! They have a special technique which lets them stay under water – they collect air at the water's surface and carry it with them as a bubble which lets them breathe underwater.

 I - SPY points: 15

POND SKATER

Pond skaters use surface tension to literally walk on water! The tiny hairs on their feet repel the water and allow them to skate across the surface. These hairs also help them find their prey – they sense vibrations and ripples on the water's surface, helping the pond skater detect insects which have fallen in.

 I - SPY points: 15

FROGSPAWN

The black balls are the eggs which are surrounded by a protective jelly that also stops them drying out. A female frog can lay up to 2000 eggs, but only about five of these will grow up into an adult frog – late frosts can kill frogspawn and predators eat many of the eggs before they fully develop.

 I - SPY points: 20

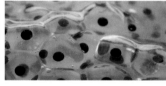

TOADSPAWN

Toad spawn is easily recognisable because it forms long strings of eggs, a bit like a necklace, unlike frogspawn which looks like a mass of jelly.

I - SPY points: 30

TADPOLES

Frogspawn and toadspawn develop into tadpoles, which in turn start to grow legs and become froglets. When tadpoles start growing their legs they become carnivorous and if there isn't enough food around they may start to eat each other!

 I - SPY points: 30

Pond Dipping
Go pond dipping to double your points on this page
www.naturedetectives.org.uk/ispy

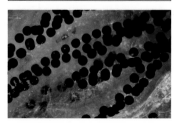

BOXING HARES

'Mad March hares' box as part of a courtship ritual in spring – it's usually the females fending off passionate males! It is also said you can see a hare in a full moon. Try it – the hare is on its back, a dark patch is its head with two 'ears' pointing away towards the right. The rest of the moon's markings make up the hare's body.

 I - SPY points: 35

SPRING LAMBS

Lambs display behaviour just like you see in school playgrounds. They will socialise and play games in groups – it's only when they get older that they spend more time alone.

 I - SPY points: 20

SLOW WORM

A slow worm is in fact a lizard, not a snake, because it has eyelids. Slow worms can live over 30 years in the wild.

 I - SPY points: 35

ADDER

In the UK a female adder will be in hibernation for 150 to 180 days of the year. The diet of an adder consists mainly of small mammals, such as mice, voles and shrews, as well as lizards.

 I - SPY points: 35

LESSER CELANDINE

This is one of the first flowers to appear at the end of winter, brightening up forest floors with a carpet of yellow 'stars' between February and May. It has narrow, pointed petals which close up before rain and at night-time. It also has dark green, heart-shaped leaves.

I - SPY points: 15

ASH

The ash tree's flowers look a bit like purple brains, or coral, exploding out of the black buds! They appear in April, before the leaves appear – the ash tree is one of the UK's last native trees to come into leaf.

I - SPY points: 15

WOOD SORREL

Wood sorrel mostly grows in woodlands and hedgerows. The white, pink-tinged flowers are very delicate and fold themselves up during rain and at night to protect the pollen inside. This is thought to be why it is sometimes known as 'sleeping beauty'.

I - SPY points: 15

WOOD ANEMONE

The wood anemone is one of the first spring flowers to appear on the woodland floor, forming a carpet of dazzling white flowers from March to May. Wood anemone spreads very slowly, so it's often a sign of an ancient woodland. If you find it in a meadow or hedgerow, it might indicate a forest used to be there many years ago – for this reason the flower is sometimes known as a 'woodland ghost'.

I - SPY points: 15

 Colour
Can you find petals in all the colours of the rainbow? Play colour bingo to double your points on this page
www.naturedetectives.org.uk/ispy

EARLY PURPLE ORCHID

This flower mostly grows in woodlands. In folklore, the early purple orchid is associated with love and was often used in love potions. The flowers are a vivid pink/purple colour and the leaves are green with dark purple/black spots on them.

I - SPY points: 20

BIRD'S-FOOT TREFOIL

This plant is often known as 'bacon and eggs' because of the yellow, red and orange colours of the flowers. It is mostly found in grassland areas and blooms between April and September.

 I - SPY points: 15

BUGLE

This plant was thought to be a cure-all by Medieval herbalists, who thought it helped to heal everything from broken bones to ulcers! One of its many nicknames – Carpenter's Herb – relates to the fact that it can help stem bleeding, so is believed to be good for healing cuts.

 I - SPY points: 15

WOOD AVENS

Folklore has it that this was one of the most powerful charms against evil spirits. Plants hung over the door were believed to be able to stop the devil entering the house!

 I - SPY points: 15

DANDELION

After a dandelion has flowered, it produces a round seed head known as a 'clock' containing up to 200 seeds, each one is shaped a little like a parachute which helps them blow away in the wind. The sap inside a dandelion stem makes a great invisible ink – perfect for writing secret messages!

 I - SPY points: 15

> **Invisible!**
> Double your points on this page by writing a secret message in invisible dandelion ink! Find out how here
> *www.naturedetectives.org.uk/ispy*

FOXGLOVE

Foxgloves produce between 20-80 magenta flowers on each stem, with each flowerhead lasting about a week. The plant is poisonous, as indicated by one of its common names 'dead man's bells'. Despite it being toxic the foxglove is also the source of an important drug, Digitalin, which is used in very small doses to treat heart disease.

I - SPY points: 15

PEACOCK BUTTERFLY

The name comes from the 'eyes' on the wings which look similar to those on a peacock's tail and scare off predators such as birds. Peacock butterflies like to feast on nectar from thistles and buddleia, as well as rotting fruit in autumn!

I - SPY points: 25

 Picnic Pack
Go on a picnic to double your points on this page. Download a free pack of recipes, games and ideas at *www.naturedetectives.org.uk/ispy*

BABY BIRDS

Watch out for adult birds flying to and from nests, bringing food for their young. Most birds bring back insects and worms to feed their babies, but some seed eating birds also regurgitate seed to help the digestion of the youngsters.

I - SPY points: 25

RED-TAILED BUMBLEBEE

Red-tailed bumblebees usually nest underground, but you'll often see them buzzing around gardens and grasslands that are rich in clover, drinking the sweet nectar.

I - SPY points: 15

KINGFISHER

These bright turquoise and orange birds perch next to slow moving or still water, looking for food. When the right moment comes along they swiftly dive into the water, catching a fish with their long beaks. They also eat aquatic insects.

I - SPY points: 25

OAK

The English oak is probably the most common British tree. It doesn't reach its full height until it's at least 150 years old and can live for 1,000 years or more.

 I - SPY points: 5

LIME

Lime trees have distinctive heart-shaped leaves. The common lime was planted so often in towns and parks in the 17th century that it gained the name 'common' as a result.

 I - SPY points: 20

HAZEL

Hazel branches are really flexible, especially in spring when green branches can even be tied into a knot!

 I - SPY points: 20

FIELD MAPLE

Field maple seeds are also known as 'helicopter' seeds and are shaped so they spin as they fall, this helps carry the seeds as far as possible in the wind, allowing new trees to grow in other locations.

 I - SPY points: 10

BEECH

Few flowers can grow in beech woods during the summer because of the deep shade cast by the trees and the thick carpet of fallen leaves.

I - SPY points: 5

HORSE CHESTNUT

The world conker championships have been held in Northamptonshire every year since 1965. The name 'horse chestnut' supposedly comes from the practice of feeding conkers to horses to cure them of illness.

 I - SPY points: 10

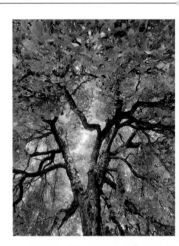

ROWAN

The rowan tree is steeped in history and mythology – rowan timber was used by Druids to make staffs and magic wands due to its straightness. It was also traditionally used for tool-handles, cartwheels and beams as it's very strong.

I - SPY points: 10

HAWTHORN

Keep an eye out for the hawthorn's white blossom in late spring – when it appears it is a good sign that summer is on the way. It is also said that hawthorn flowers smell like rotten flesh. Give them a sniff, what do you think they smell like?

 I - SPY points: 15

Leaf
Double your points on these two pages – make a leaf bag and collect all five of these leaves
www.naturedetectives.org.uk/ispy

HOLLY

The tradition of decorating the house with holly during winter goes back thousands of years. Hanging holly was thought to ward off evil spirits; it was said to be particularly effective against witches and goblins!

 I - SPY points: 15

SILVER BIRCH

With its slender trunk, silver bark and fluttering leaves, the silver birch is often called the 'Lady of the Woods'. You'll often see fly agaric in autumn (the spotty, red toadstool) growing at the base of silver birch where it feeds on the roots.

 I - SPY points: 25

LONDON PLANE

You'll often see London plane trees lining the streets of towns and cities because they are particularly tolerant of urban conditions, shedding flakes of polluted bark to leave a 'dappled' appearance to their trunks – a bit like army camouflage.

 I - SPY points: 20

WHITE POPLAR

The bark of a white poplar tree has very distinctive diamond-shaped markings, called lenticels, which help to identify it all year round.

I - SPY points: 25

SWEET CHESTNUT

Older sweet chestnuts are very recognisable because the bark develops swirly ridges, which spiral up the tree a bit like a helter-skelter. They are also usually magnificent in size, with many having huge hollow trunks that several people can fit into at once!

I - SPY points: 20

You will find fungi and mushrooms in most wooded areas. They are great to look at but can be very poisonous so please don't touch any or you could get very ill.

FLY AGARIC

This poisonous toadstool, which often appears in fairytales and stories, mostly grows at the base of birch trees. The red cap is covered in white spots, which are sometimes washed off by the rain.

 I - SPY points: 25

CHICKEN OF THE WOODS

This is a bracket fungus and it grows in shelf-like layers. It is commonly found from late spring through to autumn, often on oak trees where it causes rot which can result in hollowing.

 I - SPY points: 40

CHANTERELLE

This funnel-shaped fungus grows in woodlands, often growing in the same spot year after year. It's the colour of apricots and smells a bit like them too!

I - SPY points: 25

JELLY EAR

This fungus grows on dead trees, mostly elder, and looks like rubbery brown ears. It shrinks down to hard, dark lumps in dry weather – then transforms back to 'ears' when it rains.

I - SPY points: 30

PINK WAXCAP

The pink waxcap is also known as the ballerina – as it gets older the pink cap flattens and splits, with the edges often flicking up like a tutu.

I - SPY points: 30

WOODLAND TRUST

 MICHELIN

GIANT PUFFBALL

These huge mushrooms can grow bigger than a person's head and contain up to 7 trillion spores. They grow in grassy areas – often in rings – and burst once they mature, releasing the spores in a dusty cloud.

I - SPY points: 35

KING ALFRED'S CAKES

Insects and other small animals often make their home in this fungus. As it grows old it gets a hard, shiny, black crust like burnt buns and can be used for lighting fires as it burns like charcoal.

 I - SPY points: 40

SHAGGY INKCAP

This fungus has amazing strength and can even push its way through tarmac! It drips black ink from the edges of its cap – ink made from this mushroom was used to sign the Magna Carta in 1215.

I - SPY points: 35

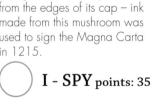

YELLOW BRAIN

This grows on dead branches and is parasitic, meaning it feeds off other fungi. Its bright yellow colour makes it easy to spot after wet weather, where it looks like yellow brains spilling out!

 I - SPY points: 30

 Fungus Trump Cards

Play top trumps to double your points on this page – get free fungus trump cards at **www.naturedetectives.org.uk/ispy**

ORANGE PEEL FUNGUS

This fungus belongs to the 'cup' family. It has fragile, thin flesh which splits easily so it looks like discarded orange peel.

I - SPY points: 35

ACORN

An oak tree doesn't usually produce a large amount of acorns until it reaches 40-50 years old. The number of acorns changes each year, but every three to five years they will produce a bumper crop of up to 50,000 acorns! This is known as a mast year.

 I - SPY points: 5

ELDERBERRY

The Romans used elderberry juice as hair dye! Elder branches also make fantastic pea shooters – they are light and filled with pith, which can be hollowed out easily.

I - SPY points: 5

ROWAN BERRY

Rowan berries can be made into jams and jellies, but they are very bitter raw. They are packed with vitamin C and a great winter food for birds, especially redwings and blackbirds.

I - SPY points: 10

 Conkers
Double up! Play conkers to double your points on this page – get championship-winning tips at
 www.naturedetectives.org.uk/ispy

CONKER

Conkers is a game traditionally played in playgrounds. You search for a really hard conker with no cracks, then attach it to the end of a piece of string and hit it against your opponent's conker, battling to see whose conker is the hardest and the champion.

I - SPY points: 5

ASH KEY

The ash tree can grow up to 30metres (98ft) in height. It grows clusters of 'keys' or winged seeds in autumn, which are swept away by the wind. The wood from ash trees is very strong and flexible, so it is often used to make furniture, tool handles, even hockey sticks.

HAZELNUTS

Hazelnuts are eaten by both people and animals. Squirrels and mice help hazel to spread by collecting the nuts, burying them, then forgetting about them so they grow into trees.

I - SPY points: 10

I - SPY points: 10

BLACKTHORN

The fruits of the blackthorn are called sloes and although they aren't poisonous they are extremely sour. Cooked sloes can be used to make jams, jellies and wine.

○ I - SPY points: 15

Seed Planting Kit
Plant a seed to double your points on this page. Get a seed planting kit crammed with ID sheets, instructions and activities at www.naturedetectives.org.uk/ispy

HAWTHORN

Hawthorn is a very common hedgerow shrub. The berries are known as haws and are eaten by many birds and mammals. Lots of animals also make their homes or nests within hawthorn hedges.

○ I - SPY points: 15

HEDGEHOG

The hedgehog's diet of pests like slugs and snails makes it a popular visitor with gardeners. It also eats beetles and earthworms, feasting throughout early autumn to store up enough energy to hibernate through winter.

 I - SPY points: 40

STAG

During autumn, the 'rutting' or mating season starts. Stags pursue groups of female deer, bellowing loudly to drive away other males that might be interested. Sometimes stags will fight each other, clashing their antlers together in a battle to see who is superior.

I - SPY points: 30

BATS

Bats are the only mammals that can fly. They are nocturnal, so they mostly sleep during the day and come out at night. All UK bats eat insects – the common pipistrelle can eat as many as 3,000 in one night!

I - SPY points: 35

FOX

Fox coats look their best in autumn, when the adults' fur has grown back after the summer moult. Foxes are scavengers and eat almost anything – from birds to insects, small mammals to autumn berries, even scraps from dustbins and can be found in many town and cities.

I - SPY points: 30

WOODLAND
TRUST

FULL MOON

The full moon is a lunar phase occurring when the moon is on the opposite side of the earth from the sun and all three bodies are aligned in a straight line.
It appears as an entire circle in the sky. The only month that can occur without a full moon is February.

 I - SPY points: 10

SPIDER WEB

Spiders produce super strong, flexible silk to spin webs and catch prey. When an insect gets trapped in the sticky web and struggles, the spider is alerted by vibrations travelling along the silky threads. The spider then wraps their prey up in silk before eating them.

 I - SPY points: 5

TREE SILHOUETTE

Look out for dead trees standing out amongst their leafy neighbours. These standing dead trees, known as 'snags', are important sources of food and shelter to a wide range of wildlife including fungi, insects, bats and birds.

 I - SPY points: 10

CROW

The crow is one of our most intelligent birds. They tend to prefer their own company to being part of a group, so look out for them on their own. They eat almost anything, including insects, seeds, fruits and dead animals.

I - SPY points: 5

WOODLAND TRUST

 MICHELIN

MIST

Mist is made up of lots of tiny water droplets suspended in the air. It is very similar to fog, in fact the difference between the two types depends on how dense they are and how this affects visibility – fog is denser with less visibility, mist is less dense with more visibility.

 I - SPY points: 15

Spooky Scavenger
Double your points on this page by going on a spooooky scavenger hunt. Get the tick list of eerie items at www.naturedetectives.org.uk/ispy

STARLINGS

Starlings flock together in an attempt to make themselves safe from predators. This flocking is called a 'murmuration' and often involves thousands of birds swooping and soaring together. So many starlings roosted on the hands of London's Big Ben in 1949 that they stopped the famous clock!

 I - SPY points: 35

SPIDER

In early autumn male spiders start scurrying around looking for a mate, so this is why you might suddenly notice more around your house at this time of year. They much prefer living outdoors though, so if you find one carefully capture it and put it back outside.

 I - SPY points: 5

COMPLETE SILENCE

Try and find somewhere you can sit in silence for a couple of minutes – it's tricky, you'll probably still be able to hear birdsong, insects or a whisper of wind. In fact the only place there is true silence is outer space – this is because it's a vacuum and sounds cannot travel in a vacuum.

I - SPY points: 20

SNOWFLAKE

Snowflakes form up in the clouds and their intricate shapes vary depending on how high they form, as well as the temperature, humidity and dirt in the air. See how many snowflakes you can catch next time it snows. How quickly do they melt?

I - SPY points: 10

ICICLES

Icicles form when water drips from an object and freezes because the air temperature is below zero degrees Celsius. Look out for icicles hanging from tree branches in cold, frosty woods.

I - SPY points: 20

FROZEN PUDDLE

Spare a thought for thirsty birds when the weather is very cold – as streams, puddles and ponds freeze over birds lose vital sources of water for drinking and bathing. You can help by putting a bird bath in your garden, keeping it topped up with fresh, clean water and breaking any ice that forms.

I - SPY points: 10

 Ice Decorations
Cold weather is fantastic for making ice decorations and they're really easy to make. Find out how and double your points on this page
www.naturedetectives.org.uk/ispy

FRESH SNOW

Freshly fallen snow is brilliant for playing in! As snow falls, it gets blown about by the wind which can cause snow drifts, as well as the 'spray-on' effect like the beech tree trunks.

I - SPY points: 15

DEER

Deer are 'ungulates', which means they have split hooves. They leave distinctive 'two-toed' prints in mud and snow. They also have long legs with powerful muscles which help them to run fast and jump.

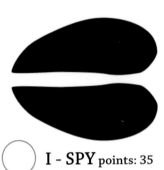

I - SPY points: 35

Animal Tracks Hunt
Double up! Hunt for more animal tracks to double your points on this page. Download the ID sheet at
www.naturedetectives.org.uk/ispy

BADGER

A badger print is similar to a dog's paw print, but you can tell them apart because a badger has five toes and a sausage shaped pad at the back.

I - SPY points: 40

SQUIRREL

Squirrels don't hibernate in winter because they can't store enough energy to sleep for such a long period. Instead they build a large drey to cosy up in and only venture out to find nuts and other items they buried in autumn. They leave complicated tracks, a mixture of claws and pads.

 I - SPY points: 25

WELLIES

Wellies get their name from the 1st Duke of Wellington, who had his shoemaker design a more comfortable, hard-wearing style of boot than had previously existed. Today they are waterproof, usually made from rubber and come in every colour and pattern imaginable – great for jumping in puddles!

 I - SPY points: 5

ASH

Ash twigs are grey with large, velvety-black pointy buds. Did you know the ash tree belongs to the olive family?

I - SPY points: 10

 Winter Twigs
Build a tower of twigs to double your points on this page. Have a competition – who can build the tallest? Get ideas at www.naturedetectives.org.uk/ispy

BEECH

Beech twigs often grow in a zig-zag shape, with long, brown torpedo-shaped buds at alternate points. Beech trees produce dense foliage, which falls to the ground in autumn creating a thick carpet of leaves.

I - SPY points: 10

HORSE CHESTNUT

Another name for the large, sticky buds found on horse chestnut twigs is 'cacky monkeys'! Look out for horseshoe shaped marks on the twigs, left by the previous year's leaves.

I - SPY points: 10

FIELD MAPLE

The field maple is the only maple tree that is native to the UK. It is also the only maple whose leaves do not turn orange or red in autumn – instead they change to a golden yellow. Buds grow in pairs on opposite side of the twigs.

I - SPY points: 10

VisitWoods is the Woodland Trust's brand new website which you can use to find your nearest wood. There are over 14,000 woodlands listed across the UK, great places to visit if you need help ticking off some of your I-SPY spots.
Visit www.VisitWoods.org.uk to find a wood with...

SAPLINGS

Heartwood Forest will one day become the biggest native forest in England. 600,000 saplings will be planted on the site in total, all by volunteers. Wildflower meadows and a community orchard will also be created.

 I - SPY points: 15

A FANTASTIC VIEW

Carnmoney Hill is one of a chain of hills that overlook Belfast in Northern Ireland. It is home to lots of wildlife including long-eared owls, sparrowhawks and Irish hares.

 I - SPY points: 15

A RIVER

Nidd Gorge is a fantastic wood which runs alongside the river Nidd, its steep slopes carved out of the North Yorkshire landscape. Watch out for kingfishers, dragonflies, otters and herons near the water's edge.

 I - SPY points: 25

Visit a Wood
Explore a wood then post a photo or comment about your adventure online to double your points on this page.
Find a woodland near you at
www.naturedetectives.org.uk/ispy

MAGICAL CREATURES

Woods are special places, home to all sorts of weird and wonderful flora and fauna. Pressmennan Wood in Scotland is home to the 'Glingbobs and Tootflits' – these elusive creatures live in the trees, they are very shy but you might see their tiny doors and windows!

 I - SPY points: 45

Index

First published by Michelin Maps and Guides 2011 © Michelin, Proprietaires-Editeurs 2011. Michelin and the Michelin Man are registered Trademarks of Michelin. Created and produced by Blue Sky Publishing Limited. All rights reserved. No part of this publication may be reproduced, copied or transmitted in any form without the prior consent of the publisher.

Print services by FingerPrint International Book production – fingerprint@pandora.be. The publisher gratefully acknowledges the contribution of the I-Spy team: Danielle Evans, Chris Hickman, Rhiannon Bates, Sarah Nicholson, Camilla Lovell, Geoff Watts and Ruth Neilson in the production of this title.

The publisher gratefully acknowledges the contribution of WTPL/Anna Badley, Margaret Barton, Stuart Michael Bateson, Bruce Beattie, Richard Becker, Niall Benvie, Daniel Billingham, Bob Carter, Diana Cave, Paul Robert Clark, Simon Clark, Ian Edwards, Danielle Evans, Karen Fisher, Dave Foker, Paul Foster, Stuart Handley, Fran Hitchinson, Pete Holmes, Albert Edward Horton, Katherine Jaiteh, Ian Jamison, EA Janes, Steven Kind, Ken Leslie, David Lund, Chris Marsh, Christine Martin, Deborah Morris, Shaun Nixon, Libby Owen, Judith Parry, Patrick Roper, Nicholas Spurling, Carole Sutton, Gwilym Thomas, Michael Turner, Keith Walkling, Lindsay Williams, Adrian Yeo, iStockphoto/Peter Booth, Mike Cherim, Marcus Clackson, Bart Coenders, Valerie Crafter, Rudd de Mann, Doctor Bass, Christopher Ermel, Trevor Fisher, Tommy Her, Andrew Howe, Laurie Knight, Elena Korenbaum, Lezh, Alexander Limbach, Florian Loebermann, Mattabe, Graeme Purdy, Vinicius Ramalho, Jon Tarrant, Jamie Van Buskirk, Ana Vasileva, cambridge2000.com, BartCo and Roger Whiteway provided the photographs in this book. Other images in the public domain and used under a creative commons licence. All logos, images, designs and image rights are © the copyright holders and are used with kind thanks and permission.

Reprinted 2014   12 11 10 9 8 7 6 5 4

HOW TO GET YOUR
I-SPY CERTIFICATE AND
BADGE

*Every time you score 1000 points
or more in an I-Spy book, you can
apply for a certificate*

HERE'S WHAT TO DO, STEP BY STEP:

Certificate

- Ask an adult to check your score

- Ask his or her permission to apply
  for a certificate

- Apply online to
  www.ispymichelin.com

- Enter your name and address and
  the completed title

- We will send you back via e mail
  your certificate for the title

Badge

- Each I-Spy title has a cut out (page
  corner) token at the back of the book

- Collect five tokens from different
  I-Spy titles

- Put Second Class Stamps on two
  strong envelopes

- Write your own address on one
  envelope and put a £1 coin inside it (for
  protection). Fold, but do not seal the
  envelope, and place it inside the second
  envelope

- Write the following address on the
  second envelope, seal it carefully and
  post to:

I-Spy Books
Michelin Maps and Guides
Hannay House
39 Clarendon Road
Watford
WD17 1JA

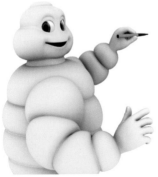